Marvellous Minibeasts!

A+ books

BREATHTAKING Beetles

by Catherine Ipcizade

Consultant:
Laura Jesse
Director, Plant and Insect Diagnostic Clinic
Iowa State University Extension
Ames, Iowa, USA

• • •

raintree
a Capstone company — publishers for children

Raintree is an imprint of Capstone Global Library Limited, a company incorporated in England and Wales having its registered office at 7 Pilgrim Street, London, EC4V 6LB – Registered company number: 6695582

www.raintree.co.uk
myorders@raintree.co.uk

ISBN 978 1 4747 3602 2 (hardback)   ISBN 978 1 4747 3606 0 (paperback)
20 19 18 17 16   21 20 19 18 17
10 9 8 7 6 5 4 3 2 1   10 9 8 7 6 5 4 3 2 1

British Library Cataloguing in Publication Data
A full catalogue record for this book is available from the British Library.

Editorial credits
Editor, Abby Colich; Designer, Bobbie Nuytten; Media Researcher, Jo Miller; Production Specialist, Tori Abraham

Acknowledgements
Alamy: blickwinkel, cover, blickwinkel/Kottmann, 11, Graphic Science, 19, imageBROKER/Alexandra Laube, 23, Robert Shantz, 9; Dreamstime: Galinasavina, 10; Minden Pictures: Mitsuhiko Imamori, 30 (molt), MYN/John Tiddy, 17, Nature Production/Kazuo Unno, 20; Newscom: Minden Pictures/Mark Moffett, 24, Minden Pictures/Thomas Marent, 14, Photoshot/NHPA/Robert Pickett, 12; Science Source: James H. Robinson, 30 (eggs, larva, pupa, adult), Stuart Wilson, 8; Shutterstock: A.S.Floro, 26, Cosmin Manci, 27, Dennis van de Water, 22, EarnestTse, 5 (bottom left), Imladris, 4, Katarina Christenson, 16, khlongwangchao, 5 (top), Liew Weng Keong, 25, macrowildlife, 7, Nicola Dal Zotto, 21, Paolo Costa, 1, photowind, 28, Puwadol Jaturawutthichai, map (throughout), RODINA OLENA, back cover (background), Sarah2, 6, seiyoh, 15, Trifecta, 18, TTstudio, 29, Weblogiq, 5 (bottom right); SuperStock: agf photo, 13

Printed and bound in India.

Contents

Beetles are **breathtaking!**

A colourful insect sits on a flower. Its shiny wings open wide. It flies away. Another insect scurries by. It can't fly. But it is bright and colourful. These insects are beetles.

Some, but not all, beetles are dull and brown. Others are bright colours. They have fun patterns. Some are shiny. Beetles truly are breathtaking.

Bee beetle

RANGE: Europe

LENGTH: 1 centimetre (0.4 inches)

BREATHTAKING FEATURE: Looks like a bee

Look at that black and yellow bug!
It is fuzzy too. It is sitting on a flower.
Is it a bee? Look again! This bug is a
beetle. Why does it look like a bee?
Some animals mimic other animals.
They may do this to protect themselves.
A predator might think this beetle is a
stinging bee. It stays away.

Blue fungus beetle

RANGE: Parts of the United States, northern Mexico

LENGTH: 1.5 cm (0.6 in.)

BREATHTAKING COLOUR: Blue or purple

It's a blue bug! The blue fungus beetle also has black dots on its body. This bug lives in forests. Females lay eggs on rotting wood. Black and white larvae hatch. They feast on fungus that grows nearby. Adults eat fungus too. Fungus is this beetle's favourite food!

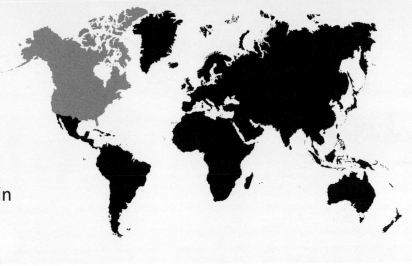

RANGE: Parts of Canada and the United States

LENGTH: 1.5 cm (0.6 in.)

BREATHTAKING FACT: Lays eggs in beehives

Can a beetle look like a chequerboard? The checkered beetle does! It is black with bright red bands. It is hairy too! What else is interesting about this bug? It lays eggs in beehives. Larvae hatch from the eggs. Then the larvae eat the bees' eggs and larvae. As adults, these beetles eat pollen from flowers.

Domino beetle

RANGE: India

LENGTH: 4 cm (1.6 in.)

BREATHTAKING DEFENCE:
  Squirts acid

What game piece does this bug look like? A domino! The domino beetle lives in deserts and other dry areas. It uses long legs to run quickly. Its legs also raise its body away from hot sand. How does this beetle protect itself? By squirting acid! Predators nearby should watch out.

Eupholus **weevils**

RANGE: New Guinea

LENGTH: 3.2 cm (1.3 in.)

BREATHTAKING COLOURS:
Bright blues and greens

Look at this bright bug! Eupholus weevils come in shades of blue and green. The colours warn predators to stay away. Most eupholus weevils eat yam leaves. The leaves are toxic to other animals.

Feather-horned beetle

RANGE: Australia

LENGTH: 2.5 cm (1 in.)

BREATHTAKING FEATURE: Feathery antennae

Are those feathers? No! They are the feather-horned beetle's antennae. Males use the antennae to track a female's scent. But there is more to see on this bug. It has dark grey or black wings. The wings are covered with white dots. Its underside is covered with hair!

antenna

Fiddler beetle

Look at this bug's markings. Do you see the shape of a fiddle or violin? The fiddler beetle doesn't play music. But it certainly looks stunning! Its home is rotting wood. When larvae hatch, they eat the wood. Adults feast on pollen and nectar from flowers.

RANGE: Australia

LENGTH: 2 cm (0.8 in.)

BREATHTAKING FEATURE: Yellow or
  green markings

Frog-legged beetle

RANGE: Southeast Asian Islands

LENGTH: 5 cm (2 in.)

BREATHTAKING FEATURE: Legs that look like a frog's

Is that a tiny frog? No. It's the frog-legged beetle. Its hind legs look like a frog's. But this bug doesn't jump. It climbs plant stems. Tiny hairs on its legs help it to hold on tightly. What is even more breathtaking? This beetle's bright green colour seems to change in the light.

Giraffe **weevil**

RANGE: Madagascar

LENGTH: 2.5 cm (1 in.)

BREATHTAKING FEATURE: Long neck

Whoa! Look at that neck! A male giraffe weevil's neck is longer than its body. Males stick out their necks and fight one another. Females have shorter necks. They use their necks to make nests. They roll up a leaf into a tube. Then they lay an egg inside.

Golden tortoise beetle

beetle after mating

What is that shiny bug? It's the golden tortoise beetle! This tiny bug is smaller than a pea. Its gold body is flecked with small dots. Some people call it "goldbug". When the beetle mates, it changes colour. It turns red, brown or orange. It may even get black spots!

RANGE: North and South America

LENGTH: 0.7 cm (0.3 in.)

BREATHTAKING COLOUR: Gold

Jewel beetles

This bug is a gem! The jewel beetle sparkles in the light. It is also called the metallic wood-boring beetle. It lives in forests. Adults feast on plant leaves, pollen and nectar. Larvae eat dead or dying wood.

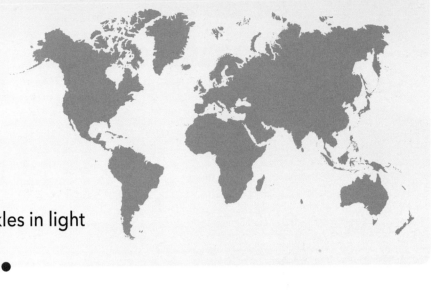

RANGE: Worldwide

LENGTH: Up to 8 cm (3.2 in.)

BREATHTAKING FEATURE: Sparkles in light

antennae

RANGE: Europe

LENGTH: 3.8 cm (1.5 in.)

BREATHTAKING FEATURE: Long antennae

Are those horns? No! They are the rosalia longicorn's antennae. A male's antennae can be longer than its body. Look at those black stripes on the antennae. They are actually hair!

Chirp! This beetle makes noise when it rubs its legs and wings together.

hair

Life cycle of a beetle

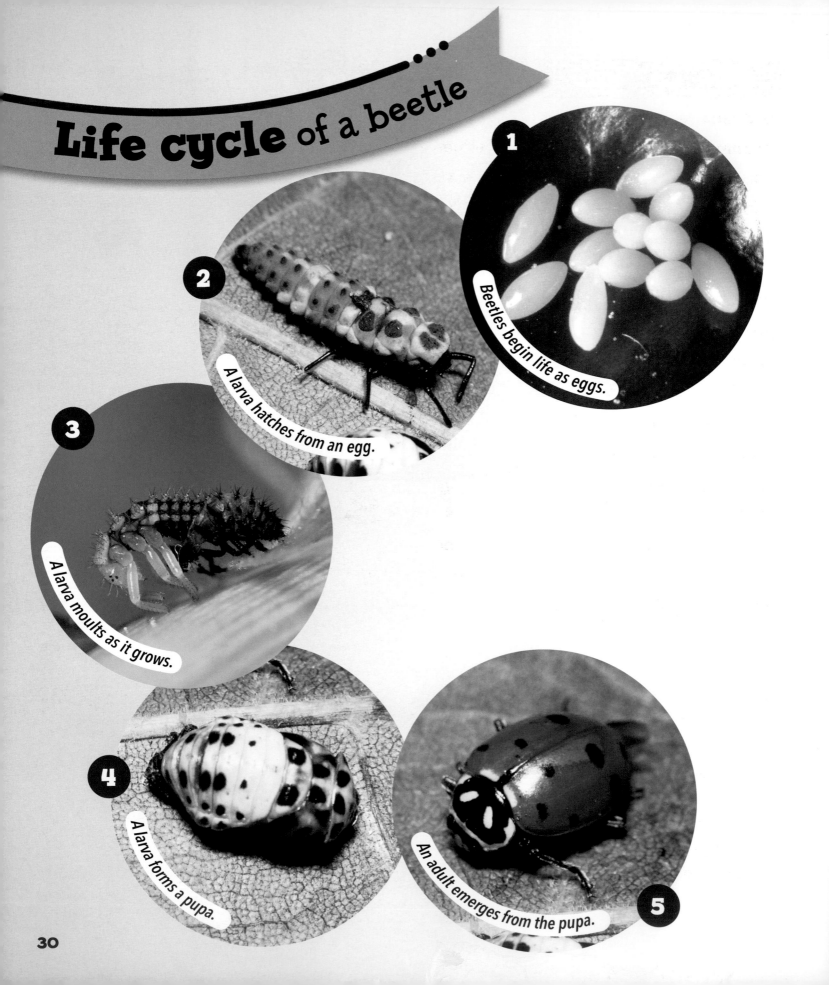

1 Beetles begin life as eggs.

2 A larva hatches from an egg.

3 A larva moults as it grows.

4 A larva forms a pupa.

5 An adult emerges from the pupa.

Glossary

antenna feeler on an insect's head

feature important part or quality of something

fungus type of organism that has no leaves, flowers or roots

larva insect at a stage of development between egg and adult

mate join together to produce young

mimic copy the look, actions or behaviours of another plant or animal

moult shed the hard outer covering while growing

nectar sweet liquid that some insects collect from flowers and eat as food

pollen tiny, yellow grains in flowers

predator animal that hunts another animal for food

range area where an animal mostly lives

toxic poisonous

Read more

Beetles (Really Weird Animals), Clare Hibbert (Franklin Watts, 2015)

British Insects (Nature Detective) Victoria Munson (Wayland, 2016)

i-SPY Creepy Crawlies (Collins, 2016)

Websites

Beetles
www.dkfindout.com/uk/animals-and-nature/insects/beetles

Fun beetle facts
www.sciencekids.co.nz/sciencefacts/animals/beetle.html

Ground beetles
www.bbc.co.uk/nature/life/Ground_beetle

Comprehension questions

1. Why do some animals mimic other animals?

2. Page 15 says yam leaves are toxic. Use the glossary on page 31 to define toxic.

3. Choose two beetles from the book. How are they alike? How are they different?

Index